Martin

by
Glynn MacNiven-Johnston

*All booklets are published thanks to the
generous support of the members of the
Catholic Truth Society*

CATHOLIC TRUTH SOCIETY
PUBLISHERS TO THE HOLY SEE

Contents

INTRODUCTION

Martin de Porres was born in 1597, in Lima, Peru. Lima at that time was a frontier town, a gold rush town, and at the same time, it was 'the pearl of the Spanish Domain'. Peru, like most of South America, was ruled as a colony of the Spanish crown. Founded in 1535, Lima had a university fewer than twenty years later, many beautiful buildings and a veneer of sophistication and culture, but the focus of most of the inhabitants was how to make money, how to make a name, how to become 'someone'. You had to be first, succeed, be respected, and every slight must be challenged; failure was an embarrassment to be hidden and ignored. Poverty was a sign of failure so the poor were despised. Everyone had to make his own way. Slavery was a large commercial venture and racism was considered normal. Society was rigidly structured. Who you were was very important. Snobbery was rife. Becoming rich was not enough, you also had to come from a noble family. First were the Spanish-born, then the whites born in Latin America and at the bottom the heap, the blacks and Amerindians.

This can seem very alien to us but our own society is less different than we might imagine, with its cult of celebrity and longing for fame and wealth, its individualism and fear of 'disrespect'. Pride is lauded, humility distrusted. We are encouraged to exaggerate our achievements and ignore our faults. We may feel guilt about the world's poor, but our day-to-day concerns probably focus on our own comfort. And so the saint that God raised up to confound sixteenth century Lima has just as much to say to us today.

BACKGROUND AND EARLY LIFE

There is no documentation of Martin's birth, but his baptism by Fr Juan Antonio Polanco was registered on Wednesday, 9th December 1597 in the Church of St Sebastian in Lima. The baptismal register, which gives his mother's name as Ana Velasquez and his godparents' names as Juan de Bribiesca and Ana de Escarcena, states 'father unknown'.

Parents

In fact Martin's father was Juan de Porres or Porras, a Spanish 'hidalgo', an elite soldier, a member of the Order of Alcantara, answering directly to the King of Spain. He had met Ana Velazquez, a freed slave, in Panama and had brought her with him to Lima. Martin was born there, followed two years later by his sister, Juana. This was a little embarrassing as 'hidalgos' were meant to be celibate during their period of service. Ana Velasquez was born in Panama but there is some speculation that her parents were brought from Senegal. Juan de Porres was possibly the son of Martin de Porras y Santodomingo from the Burgos region of Spain (the family used Porres and Porras interchangeably) but none of this can be stated for certain.

The fact that Ana was black and a freed slave meant Juan would not even have considered marrying her. There was no idea of equality in sixteenth century Peru when only a few years before there had been much debate about whether blacks and Amerindians were fully human – if they even had souls.

It is said that Juan de Porres was ashamed of Martin's dark skin but even without that neither Martin nor his sister would ever have had the same acceptance as legitimate children. The father of illegitimate children simply did not have the same kind of responsibility towards them as towards his legitimate children. Soon after Juana's birth Juan disappeared from their lives, having been sent to Santiago de Guayaquil in Ecuador. Ana struggled to bring up the children and in this Martin's soft heart and love of God did not make day to day life any easier.

Early sufferings

The virtues which marked him out as an adult, his compassion for the poor and his love of prayer, were already there in his childhood. Ana would send him out to buy food but he would give the money away, leaving his family with nothing to eat.

And, even as a small child, Martin had a deeply rooted love of prayer. He spent hours praying in the local church when his mother was expecting him back. Martin's idea of what was important did not always agree with his mother's and it is little wonder that she often beat him.

When Martin was eight years old and Juana six, Juan suddenly re-appeared and decided to acknowledge his children. He took them, without Ana, back to Ecuador where he provided them with an education. He even introduced them as his children to his relatives. After a short time Juan was transferred to Panama. He did not take the children with him. Juana remained in Ecuador with the family of a relative, Diego Marcos de Miranda, while Martin was sent back to Lima. For some reason he did not go back to his mother but went to board with a woman called Ventura de Luna near the St Lazarus Hospital in the Malambo district of Lima, a poor neighbourhood which contained the pens where slaves were imprisoned while they waited to be sold. Lima became an increasingly important slave port in the sixteenth century and by the time of Martin's death, half the population of Lima was black.

Attachment to Christ

Martin was only around ten or eleven years old but he was living independently and alone, renting a room and going out to work to support himself. He was apprenticed to a barber-surgeon, Marcelo de Rivero, who became a lifelong friend. Barber-surgeons, as well as cutting hair and shaving, set bones, treated wounds, pulled teeth, and let blood. Martin also learned herbal medicine from a man called Mateo Pastor. Martin had a gift for healing and people came to him from all over the city despite the fact that he was still little more than a child.

It was at this point in his life that others began to see his love of prayer, his devotion to the suffering Christ and his desire to share in that suffering. Martin often asked his landlady for discarded candle stubs to light his room at night. He asked for so many she became curious and looked through his door to find him in prayer in front of the crucifix his arms outstretched tears running down his face. Why did he do this? Was it out of sentimentality? He remained like this for hours night after night. Even the most sentimental person usually gives up after a time because of the discomfort if nothing else. Perhaps it was loneliness. If so, in turning to Christ he showed discernment well beyond his years. Looking at his later life though, it seems reasonable to assume that he had already entered into that intense relationship with Christ which marked his whole life. He was with Christ in prayer, offering up his own sufferings to complete Christ's suffering; and he already understood and was overwhelmed by Christ's love for him. Whatever it was, it so impressed Ventura de Luna that she called her neighbours to come and see too and Martin's reputation for holiness spread.

LIFE AS A DOMINICAN

When he was fifteen, Martin wanted to enter the Dominican Priory of Our Lady of the Rosary. He joined as a *donate*. This literally means 'someone who is a gift' but in those days a donate was basically a servant member of the community. In fact it was impossible for him to be accepted as a friar. Even the Church had not escaped the pervading racism of contemporary society. One rule stated, 'nowhere in the provinces of the Indies may there ever be received into the holy habit and profession of our Order…those who are begotten on either side of Indian or African blood'. It seems that Martin's father, who was now Governor of Panama, was furious that his son should spend his life doing the menial work considered beneath the professed brothers. He put some pressure on the Order to have Martin accepted as a lay brother and it may be that in the end it was Martin himself who refused, preferring to imitate Christ in taking the last place. Whatever the reason Martin remained a servant, at least until 1603 when he may have been professed as a lay brother, though there is some dispute over this. He was happy, at peace and in the will of God.

He was happy to be the least among the brothers. He saw himself as unworthy not because he was black and illegitimate but because he was truly Christian. He was not comparing himself with other men based on their worldly status but, as St Paul says, considering the other person better than himself (*Phil* 2:3).

Taking the last place

In a society where status was everything, Martin sought none. At one point the priory was very short of money and the Prior decided to sell some of the statues and paintings from the church. Martin was upset that Christ's house should lose some of its glory and he suggested to the Prior that he, Martin, should be sold instead. After all, he said, since he was a donate, he was the property of the order. Martin did not offer this lightly nor was he being dramatic or seeking attention. Slavery was not seen as morally wrong by the majority of people and slaves could fetch large sums of money. The Prior did not accept but Martin was able to offer this because he knew that 'nothing can come between us and the love of Christ' (*Rom* 8:35). His relationship with Christ was so profound that he was able to see that nothing else mattered.

In the priory, Martin's duties were to sweep the cells and cloisters and to clean the toilets. These were not water closets but earth closets where the contents had to be scooped out and carried off in buckets. The smell alone made this work horrible but Martin did not resent it or try to avoid the work. Normally if a person had to do such a job the smell would permeate his clothes and hair but this apparently did not happen.

In a statement taken soon after Martin's death, Br Juan Ochoa de Verastegui said:

'...having seen the said servant of God involved in [cleaning the toilets] I thought that he would emit some bad smell but I always saw him as if he had never done such a duty. [He always had] a delightful smell on his person and never with a bad smell. Also although he wore a hair shirt that stripped his skin and made him sweat profusely, this witness, on embracing him, always found a delightful smell on his person, by which reason makes me consider that as one who living among sinners does not sin, the same with [Martin], working among bad smells does not smell.'

Submission to the Rule

Martin's only ambition was to be like Christ and to this end he submitted his own will to the Rule. He wanted to be free from all selfishness and egotism, and so he did only and exactly what St Dominic had said his friars should do. Since he had been a barber he was given the job of cutting his confrères' hair. There was a rule about how the hair should be cut and Martin followed it to the letter. This did not make him popular with some of the other brothers who were less stringent about obedience and vainer about their appearance. Because he was only a donate they felt free to complain and insult him. Martin accepted this with patience and gentleness but he continued to cut the brothers' hair according to the Rule and in the end everyone accepted it.

The Rule also said that habits should be made of serge, a rough woollen weave, but for some time it was impossible to get wool to make the friars' habits and they started wearing linen ones instead. Martin went out begging for wool all over Lima until he was able to get enough to make habits for all the friars. Then as the friars sent their habits to be washed he replaced them with the rough wool habits. He knew that the Rule was there to help the brothers to be free from 'self indulgent passions and desires'.

Obedience

Obedience is often misunderstood and not given much importance but, as anyone who has tried can tell you, it is very difficult to do, and yet it is fundamental to the life of a Christian. It is by Christ's obedience that we are saved and we are called to imitate him in this. Martin did. The

Prior said of him that he 'sought nothing but the will of his superiors' and that ' he obeyed with virility of soul and of his own will'. The same is true of penance. People sometimes think practices such as wearing a hair shirt are odd or masochistic. Perhaps in some cases they can be. But what is important is the spirit in which they are done, and the reason for it. For Martin, voluntary mortifications (he wore a hair shirt and a chain around his waist in imitation of St Dominic) were a way of identifying in a real, physical way with the Passion of Christ, and was all part of his desire to conform himself to Christ completely. As St Paul puts it, 'It makes me happy to suffer for you, as I am suffering now, and in my own body to do what I can to make up all that has still to be undergone by Christ for the sake of his body, the Church'. (*Col* 1:24)

Racism

Martin's holiness was not immediately recognised in the priory and he suffered racist abuse and contempt at the hands of his confrères. He was often called a 'mulatto dog' which may sound just curious to us but which was a double insult on his mixed race and 'low' birth. Martin did not resent these insults. He always said he deserved much worse and that Christ had suffered much more for him. He was happy to be able to share in the humiliation that Christ suffered for us. He showed that it is really possible to love as Christ loved, to 'live now not with my own life but with the life of Christ who lives in me' (*Gal* 2:20). He loved those who insulted him even more and the love which he had for them slowly changed them too.

Martin might sound insufferable, inhuman even, but he was not. He was quiet, he spoke very little, he kept his eyes downcast and his hands in his sleeves when he was not working but he was also full of joy. He was known for his wonderful smile.

Care of the novices

Martin had great concern for the novices. He was like a father to them. He looked after all their needs so that they only had to concentrate on their studies. And sometimes he helped them with their studies. They were dumbfounded to have this servant help them to understand Aquinas. How he could do this is a mystery since as far as we know he had never studied at all but contemporary testimonies insist it did happen.

Martin seems to have been holy from the time he was young but the same was not true of all the novices most of whom were teenagers. Amongst them there was bullying. The one who suffered most was Cypriano de Medina, the Archbishop of Mexico's nephew. He found his studies difficult. He was short and fat and very hairy. One day a group of novices was with Martin to be shaved and have their hair cut. They started mocking Cypriano and betting each other how long it would take Martin to 'barber the wild man'. Martin stopped them. One day, he said, Cypriano would tower over them all, physically and spiritually. He was proved right. Shortly afterwards Cypriano developed a serious fever and was bedridden for several months. When he was finally well he had grown very tall and lost a lot of weight. We do not know whether or not he remained hairy but that did not prevent him from becoming a bishop at a young age.

A MAN FOR OTHERS

Martin also worked with the infirmarian (the friar whose job it was to care for the sick), Br Fernando Aragones. There were 300 friars as well as the poor who came to be treated. For Martin being with the sick person was as important as the medicine itself. He would be with them all day, attending to their every need and at night he would not go to his own bed but just lie down to sleep wherever he found himself. (In fact his normal bed was just a plank and a wooden block for a pillow.) Nothing was too much trouble for Martin. He did not just treat his patients, he nursed and cosseted them. A friar recalled that when he was sick he asked Martin for an orange. Martin brought him one. It was only later, when the friar had recovered, that he realised oranges were not in season and wondered where Martin had found it.

Curing the sick

Many stories circulated of Martin's love for his patients and his ability to cure them when doctors had given up. People remembered that he would always say 'I cure you. May God heal you.' And many of his cures seemed miraculous.

Juan de Figueroa told the story of one of them. A Dominican priest, Pedro de Montesdoca, 'was sick in bed with an illness that came upon his leg… Brother Martin de Porres came to take care of him but because of some childishness, Father Pedro became angry and insulted Martin calling him mulatto dog and other bad things after which Brother Martin [left the cell laughing. The next day, Martin] with much peace and joy entered the cell with a salad of capers saying to [Father Pedro] "Well, Father, are you still angry? Eat this little salad of capers I have brought you." Father Pedro was amazed because he had wanted such a salad all day and he was so sick from this illness and suffering from hunger and also the pain of knowing that his leg was to be amputated the following day. So it seemed strange to him that [Martin] had brought him exactly what he wanted and thinking this an act of God, he asked pardon of Brother Martin for the anger and the words he had spoken and gave him thanks for the gift… [Then] he asked [Martin] to take pity on him because they were going to cut off one of his legs. At which Brother Martin…put his hand on [the leg] and Father Pedro was healed and freed from danger.'

Martin's reputation as a healer was such that he was called to care for the visiting Archbishop of Mexico, Don Feliciano de Vega, who had fallen ill. He spent hours caring for the Archbishop but he still returned to the priory to perform his usual duties. One of the friars found him cleaning the toilets and was astonished to find him doing that when he could have been at the Archbishop's palace.

Martin also treated sick and wounded people he found on the streets. At first he used to take them to his cell but when the Prior forbade this, he sent them to his sister who had married and returned to Lima. Once he found a man, who had been in a knife fight, lying outside the door of the priory. The man had been badly wounded; his intestines were actually hanging out, and, since his condition was too serious to move him, Martin took him to his cell but, because in doing this he was disobeying a direct order from his Prior, he prayed God to heal the man quickly. The man was healed overnight with only a thin scar to show where the wound had been.

Care of Orphans

At first Martin also used his sister's house for the street children and abandoned babies he found. He was much criticised for rescuing them. People did not see this as an act of charity but thought he was saving children who would grow up to be criminals, that it would be much better to leave them on the street where they might die before they grew up to be too dangerous. Later, probably to the relief of his poor sister, he founded Holy Cross orphanage and school and found teachers and carers to look after the children. He provided education and training

for the children so they could make their own way in the world and since the girls needed some help to get married he also provided dowries. He begged for the money and then trusted in God's providence which did not fail him.

He gave everything for the poor and this was sometimes uncomfortable for his relatives. He even spent the money intended for his own niece Catalina's dowry on clothes for the poor. She was distraught, as marriage without a dowry was unheard of, but Martin was not sorry or worried. He just told her she had lost nothing and he was proved correct when a rich friend of the family replaced the dowry.

Feeding the hungry

Brother Fernando Aragones, the infirmarian, witnessed to Martin's care for the poor who came to the monastery. 'Around noon, about the time to eat, the said servant of God went to the refectory and took a cup and a bowl to collect any food left from the religious who ate by his side. If he saw any poor at the door of the refectory his impatience was notable until he was able to bring them food. When he had met their need, he calmed down and ate only bread and water so that through his great abstinence more could be fed, a sign of his great charity. And after having finished eating he took his bowl and his cup full of food and went to the kitchen of the infirmary where he waited on the sick and the poor from the neighbourhood and dogs and cats which at that hour waited for sustenance from the hand of the said servant of God. And before distributing the food he would give them a blessing saying, "May God increase it through his infinite mercy." And it seems that is what happened, that God increased the food...for all ate and their bowls were filled and all were contented even the cats and dogs.'

Martin did not judge those he helped. When he came across a group of mercenaries who had found themselves destitute, he did not judge them for their profession or accuse them of being killers, he simply saw them as men who needed help and so he helped them. Every day for months he walked five miles to and from the priory in order to bring them food until they were able to provide for themselves.

When he was not working in the priory, Martin was out in the streets of Lima, visiting the sick and looking out for those who needed his help. It was in this way that he gained an assistant. He discovered Juan Vasquez living on the streets. Juan had come from Spain with his father, who had been with the Court of the Inquisition, but the father had died leaving fourteen year old Juan to fend for himself in a foreign country with no friends or contacts and literally without even a shirt on his back. Martin took him back to the Priory and, taught him barbering. Juan stayed, becoming Martin's assistant in all his charitable works.

Martin also visited the prisons. Prisoners who did not have families to help them could find themselves without food, and once, when Martin had neither food nor money to help them, he pawned his own hat so that he could at least buy them bread. And it is said that it was not only in Lima that Martin visited prisoners. A Spanish nobleman, who was visiting Lima, recognised Martin as the man who had regularly visited him in prison during the long years he was held for ransom by the Muslims in North Africa. Martin, it seems, like Padre Pio, was granted the gift of bilocation, the possibility of being in two places at the same time, since once he had entered the priory, he never left Lima.

Bilocation

He was also reportedly seen in China, Japan and France. Nearer home, his sister said that Martin appeared one day at her house while she and her husband were in the middle of a blazing row. He arrived and cheerfully announced that he had brought them fruit and wine. Then he told them he knew what they were arguing about, explained the other's point of view to each of them and sorted out the situation. The next day when she was visiting the priory, Juana told the Prior how grateful she was for Martin's visit and help. The Prior was puzzled because he knew Martin had not left the priory that day.

Then there were the new poor. These were the orphans and widows of Spanish grandees. They had once held power and wealth and were the very people who would have held someone like Martin in contempt. After the death of their husbands or fathers they had no income and became destitute. Their pride would not let them beg in public so Martin helped them in secret and, so they would not be embarrassed by accepting help from a black man, he sent his assistant Juan Vasquez. He did not judge them for their racism or their snobbery but loved them with the love Christ had for them.

Martin did not see the rich and poor as each other's enemies. He saw that some people had been made rich so that they could show and share the charity of God, and a great deal of money came his way. The Count of Chinchon, the King's Viceroy, sent him a hundred thousand pesos every month. Juan de Figueroa, the Governor, collected mass stipends for the monastery. Meals for the students and novices were paid for by another benefactor, yet another gave the income from houses she owned, and these were only a few of those who contributed to Martin's work.

Martin was known throughout Lima as 'Holy Martin', something he found very difficult.

St Francis of the Americas

These days it is for his love of animals and his ability to talk to them that Martin is best known. He is usually shown holding a broom and with a dog, a cat and a mouse at his feet. This is because not only people came to Martin to be treated. Animals came too. With Martin animals overcame their natural enmity. Animals that would normally attack or even eat each other were persuaded to eat together instead. One story tells of a time a dog a cat and a mouse all ate from the same bowl and this is the incident shown in pictures and statues. People were amazed to see the queues of sick animals patiently waiting along with the sick people and even more amazed to see animals returning when Martin told them to. If he had to stop in order to go to pray or if he wanted to check on a patient's progress, Martin would tell them to come back the next day. He said this to animals as well as people and the animals kept their appointments too.

All animals loved him and crowded round him whenever he came near. The priory's chickens flocked to him, not to be fed but to be petted. They loved to be picked up and have their feathers smoothed. Martin returned their affection. When he was dying the doctor prescribed a poultice of chicken's blood but Martin did not want one of the chickens to be killed for his sake. A cat followed him around, stayed near him while he slept and woke him every morning in time to ring the three o'clock bell - the first prayer bell of the community. Wild and dangerous animals too, trusted him and were tame with him. There are stories of a wild bull he calmed, a savage dog he tried and failed to teach not to bite, and a hawk whose wing he mended and who afterwards stayed near him.

Of mice and dogs

Perhaps the best-known animal story is about mice. It seems that mice were chewing holes in the priory's linen - altar cloths, vestments and sheets. Martin was told to set traps but instead he caught one of the mice and spoke to it, telling it that it was not acceptable for the mice to be destroying these things. He asked the mouse to gather all the other mice together and allow Martin to take them to the stables where he promised to bring them food every day. Apparently the mice agreed because they gathered as arranged and Martin made sure they always had food. This is why St Martin de Porres is invoked against infestations of mice or rats.

If it seems extreme to love God's creation in vermin, Martin went even further. When working in the fields or the garden he always worked stripped to the waist so that the mosquitoes could feed off him. Even mosquitoes, he said, deserved to eat.

Martin was especially known for his love of dogs. Whenever he went out of the monastery he brought back all the sick dogs he found and treated them with the same care as he did people. Eventually the cloister became overrun with these feral dogs and the Prior told Martin to get rid of them. Martin gathered up as many as he could and took them to his sister Juana's house. Martin's niece, Catalina, gave the following account

> 'One day my mother asked him [Martin] why he kept bringing so many dogs to her house. They made her angry since they soiled the house. He told her he was looking for a new place for them. Then he went outside and talked to the dogs telling them that when they had a necessity to go, to do it in the street outside and I saw that since that moment the dogs, when they had a necessity to go, would leave the yard and do it in the street outside and then come back without making anyone in the house angry or soiling the house like before.'

There is even testimony that Martin brought a dog back to life. The procurator of the monastery, Br Juan de Vicuna, had a dog which was eighteen years old, and was infirm, mangy and stinking. Finally Br Juan thought that the best thing would be to have it put out of its misery so he sent one of the servants to kill it. The servant smashed the

dog's head in with a large stone and was carrying the
body to throw it in the river when he met Martin and
another brother, Br Lauren. Martin took the dog back to
his own cell and put it on the floor Br Lauren solemnly
swore that the dog was dead but when Martin put it down
the dog tried to sit up. Martin sewed up its wounds and
cared for it for three days. After that, the dog returned to
Br Juan, cured and no longer smelly and mangy. Br Juan
was overjoyed to have the dog back but Martin, even
though he was 'mild and full of forbearance', told Br
Juan he should have treated his old companion better.

Like St Francis

Martin is often called the St Francis of Assisi of the
Americas and these two saints were alike in many ways.
Both loved God's whole creation and could communicate
with animals and in this they were a sign of what had
been lost by Adam and Eve's disobedience; a sign of the
whole creation waiting for salvation. And, like Francis,
Martin is often thought of as a sweet and harmless saint.
But they are also alike in the severity of their lives.
Although Francis had come from a rich family and had
lived a dissolute life before converting, he too valued
humility, poverty, obedience and penance.

Everything that Martin did, he did through prayer. All
his strength came from that deep union with God. He

used to spend hours praying in front of the Blessed Sacrament. On holy days he disappeared completely, finding solitude somewhere in the priory so that he could spend the whole day in prayer. Sometimes he levitated when praying. This was seen many times by his confrères, by Juan Vasquez and also by a small boy, Niccolo de Penasola, who later became a priest. Niccolo was hiding in the choir stalls one day, escaping from punishment at home. When he looked out he saw Martin raised high above the ground in ecstasy.

And his prayer worked miracles. When torrential rains caused the river Rimac, the river on which Lima stands, to flood, people came to Martin for help. They were afraid that a small church dedicated to Our Lady would be damaged by the rising waters. Martin went with them and knelt in front of the swollen river. He picked up three small pebbles to represent the Holy Trinity and he began to pray. As he prayed the waters receded and the church was undamaged. The people were relieved and decided to rebuild the church further away but Martin told them there was no need and to this day the church has never been flooded.

St John of Macias

Martin also had a great devotion to Our Lady. So much so that he, who had nothing for himself, had two rosaries, one to use and one to wear round his neck so that it was

always near him. This devotion was shared by his friend
Juan Macias. Juan had come to Peru from Spain in 1619
when he was thirty-four years old and had joined the
Dominicans three years later. He became a lay brother
and the doorkeeper of the Priory of St Mary Magdalene,
another of the four Dominican priories in Lima. Like
Martin he was known for his care for the poor and deep
devotion to Our Lady. Juan prayed the rosary constantly
for the souls in purgatory and when possible he and
Martin would pray together. Juan used to say that six or
seven hours in prayer only seemed to him like fifteen
minutes. We know him better as St John Macias; he was
canonised in 1975.

Juan also sought Martin's help when a young novice,
Luis Gutiérrez, almost severed a finger. During some
horseplay, Luis had snatched a fruit from the hand of a
friend not realising that his friend was holding a sharp
knife in the same hand. His finger was badly cut, even the
nerves and tendons were damaged. Because of how it had
happened, Luis did not say anything and the finger
became gangrenous. He was distraught as it seemed his
hand would have to be amputated. If losing his hand were
not bad enough in itself, he would not be able to be
ordained a priest if he only had one hand. When he heard
Martin would come, Luis was at once anxious and
hopeful. Both his hand and arm were swollen and his

finger was almost completely severed. Martin made a paste from herbs and put it into the wound, re-bandaged the hand, made the sign of the cross and left. Luis was stunned. Surely that could not be all the famed healer was going to do. But by morning the swelling had gone down and the finger had re-attached itself. His hand and his priesthood were both saved.

St Rose of Lima

Martin de Porres and John Macias were not the only saints living in Lima at that time. Rose of Lima, a Dominican tertiary who lived a life of charity and penance also lived then. Whether she and Martin knew each other is unknown but it is possible since she often attended mass at the priory and Juan de Lorenzana, the Provincial who accepted Martin into the priory, was also Rose's spiritual director. Although she died in 1617, she was only ten years older than Martin. She was canonised in 1671.

And in case there should seem to be only Dominican saints, there was also St Turibius de Mongrovejo. He was the Archbishop of Lima who confirmed both Martin and Rose. He was a great reformer of the clergy as well as a defender of the rights of the Amerindians. He travelled the whole of his diocese on foot three times and was canonised in 1726.

SICKNESS AND DEATH

In October 1639 Martin became ill, probably from typhus
(he was 42). Even on the first day of his illness he told his
friend, Fr Juan de Barbaran that he would not recover.
Martin was bedridden. The Prior insisted that Martin
allow the friars to put sheets on his bed. He accepted in
obedience but he still kept on a hair shirt and his rough
habit. During this illness he was cared for by the
Viceroy's own doctor and attended by the Archbishop,
Felician de Vega. He suffered terrible fever and pain. The
devil appeared and tried to overwhelm him with terror.
The Prior, seeing his agony and struggle, suggested
Martin call on the help of St Dominic. Martin replied that
St Dominic was already there along with St Vincent
Ferrer. He could see them in the room with him. To fight
against the attacks of the devil, Martin fixed his eyes on
the crucifix facing his bed, on the wounds of Christ. At
around eight in the evening Martin told those caring for
him that it was time to sound the wooden clappers to
summon the community to the bedside of a dying brother.
He died an hour later, on 3rd November 1639, as the
brothers of his community chanted the Creed round his
bed. Those who were there said that he simply closed his

eyes and gently died. The peace they saw on his face
inspired them and helped their grief. Archbishop de Vega
said, 'Brothers, let us learn from Brother Martin how to
die. This is the most difficult and most important lesson.'
The friars began to lay out the body. They found a new
habit waiting. Martin, who, in imitation of St Dominic,
had worn a shabby worn-out habit during his life, had
arranged a new habit to be buried in. When they clothed
his body for burial the friars were moved to tears by the
scars and weals on Martin's body, the hair shirt and the
iron chain round his waist.

Then the bells were rung to tell the people of Lima that
Martin had died.

Funeral

At the funeral Fr Cypriano de Medina, the once bullied
novice, went to the catafalque and found the body already
in rigor. He protested to Martin that the whole city was
coming to see him and he should look a bit better! He
said Martin should ask God to make him look a little less
dead. In a few moments the body lost its rigidity and
Martin began to look as he had in life. Fr Cypriano was
so overcome by the answer to his prayer that he lifted the
body into a sitting position. By four o'clock in the
morning of the funeral, people were already crowding
outside the doors of the church. As soon as the sacristan

opened the doors everyone poured inside but they
behaved well during the funeral mass. After the mass
however they all rushed up to the catafalque to touch the
body, touch devotional objects to it and snip off bits of
the habit. After the funeral the body had to be reclothed
because the habit had been ripped to shreds. Then people
started bringing the sick to touch his body and healing
miracles were already being reported.

Burial

As it got dark the brothers began to get worried by the
onslaught of the crowds and decided to bury Martin
without further delay. The body of Martin de Porres,
illegitimate, mixed race and poor, a servant in the priory,
was carried by the Viceroy, the Bishop of Cuzco, the
Archbishop of Mexico and a judge of the royal court. He
was buried in the crypt under the chapter house of the
Priory. It did not seem fitting to the friars that he should be
buried with the lay brothers so he was buried in the area
reserved for priests. They found a new niche where
another lay brother, Br Miguel de Santo Domingo, was
already buried. He too, in his lifetime, had been seen to be
very holy and so was considered worthy to be near Martin.

HOLINESS AND VIRTUE RECOGNISED

Death did not stop Martin's care for the sick. Many miracles were reported and attributed to his intercession, among them that of Fr Cypriano, who in 1643, returned to Lima from Spain where he had been a delegate at the chapter meeting. Almost immediately, he fell ill with stabbing pains in his arms and legs which were so severe he could not sleep and extreme nausea so that he could not eat at all. Within a few days his condition was critical. The doctors said nothing could be done, but the friars, remembering how close he had been to Martin, advised him to call on Martin's help and the Prior, Gasper de Saldana, sent him Martin's rosary which was placed around Fr Cypriano's neck. In the night Martin appeared to Fr Cypriano and Fr Cypriano berated him asking how Martin could just sit around in heaven while his friend was suffering. Martin just smiled and told him he wasn't going to die and in the morning Fr Cypriano was completely cured.

Nor did Martin cure only his brothers. Many other cases were reported by people all over Lima, a small boy brought back from the point of death, a woman cured of neuralgia, another cured of a serious fever and many others.

Body moved to new chapel

As devotion to Martin grew, more and more people came to the church of the Holy Rosary which was the nearest those outside the priory could get to his tomb. The brothers saw that Martin needed to be moved so that the faithful could have access to his tomb. The Prior realised that the best place would be the supply room of the infirmary. This place where Martin had worked could easily be converted into a chapel. Twenty-four years after his death Martin's body was exhumed and translated to his new resting place. The friars intended the translation to be private but word got out and crowds of people and local dignitaries arrived. The casket containing the bones was carried with great ceremony by the Viceroy of Lima as no one dared oppose him. The friars warned that people should not show outward signs of devotion to Martin since his life had not yet been judged by the church but the faithful ignored them and knelt and kissed the tomb and showed all the devotion due to a saint.

The Dominicans recognised Martin's virtue very quickly. Only two years after his death, in 1641, a solemn encomium of his life (a list of his virtues and good deeds) was pronounced at the provincial Chapter. His story spread throughout Latin America and soon reached Europe. The first biography was published in Spain in 1647 and the second in Rome in 1658. In 1659, the

Spanish King himself, Philip IV, wrote to the Holy See asking that Martin's cause be introduced.

Road to Sainthood

In 1660, the Archbishop of Lima, Pedro de Villagomez, opened the Ordinary Process for the cause of Martin de Porres. Since it was only twenty years after his death many people who had known him personally were able to testify. Pope Clement IX signed the decree for the introduction of the cause and the remissorial letters were sent but the ship carrying them sank and it was another nine years before they finally arrived in Lima.

The commission began its investigation and, since there were a hundred and sixty-eight testimonies, it took eight years to complete. At the end of the eight years the resulting acts of the Process were sent to Rome. And again the ship sank. Fortunately there was a copy of the work, which did actually arrive, but seventy-five years passed before Martin was declared Venerable.

Beatification did not happen until 1837, when two miracles were accepted. One involved a woman, Elvira Moriano, who lost an eye after a shard of pottery hit her. Her sight and her eye were restored when she held a relic of Martin to the socket. The second was the cure of a two year old boy, Melchior Verada, the son of a slave. He had been given up for dead when he fell from a balcony. After

Martin's help was invoked, the boy got up and began to play as if nothing had happened.

Martin wasn't canonised until 1962. Again two miracles were needed and again they involved a woman and a small boy. The first, in 1958, was the cure of an eighty-seven year old woman, Dorothea Calallero Escalante, a Paraguyan, who had fallen ill with an intestinal obstruction. An operation to treat it was out of the question because of her age and the doctors said nothing more could be done. Dorothea's daughter Juana was living in Argentina. As soon as she heard of her mother's condition she travelled to Paraguay to what she thought was her mother's death bed. She prayed all the way asking Martin to intercede for her so that her mother would not die before she arrived. The next day her mother had been completely cured and lived several more years

The second miraculous cure was that of four year old Antonio Cabrera Perez whose foot was crushed when a cement block fell on it. He was taken to hospital but gangrene set in and the doctors decided they had no choice but to amputate his leg. Then a family friend suggested the parents pray to Blessed Martin and so both parents and the director of the hospital spent the night invoking his help. In the morning the gangrene was gone and the foot was healed. Two years later, Antonio and his family attended the canonisation of St Martin de Porres on 6th May 1962.

Canonisation

At the Canonisation Mass Pope John XXIII gave this summary of St Martin's significance for Christians.

'The example of Martin's life is ample evidence that we can strive for holiness and salvation as Christ Jesus has shown us: first by loving God with all your heart, with all your soul and with all your mind; and second by loving your neighbour as yourself.

'When Martin had come to realise that Christ Jesus suffered for us and that he carried our sins on his body to the cross, he would meditate with remarkable ardour and affection about Christ on the cross. Whenever he contemplated Christ's terrible torture he would be reduced to tears. He had an exceptional love for the great sacrament of the Eucharist and often spent long hours in prayer before the Blessed Sacrament. His desire was to receive the sacrament in communion as often as he could.

'St Martin, always obedient and inspired by his divine teacher, dealt with his brothers with that profound love which comes from pure faith and humility of spirit. He loved men because he honestly looked on them as God's children and his own brothers and sisters. Such was his humility that he loved them even more than himself and considered them to be better and more righteous than he was.

'He excused the faults of others. He forgave the bitterest injuries, convinced that he deserved much more severe punishments on account of his own sins. He tried with all his might to redeem the guilty; lovingly he comforted the sick; he provided food, clothing and medicine for the poor; he helped, as best he could...: thus he deserved to be called by the name the people gave him: 'Martin of Charity'.

'The virtuous example and even the conversation of this saintly man exerted a powerful influence in drawing men to religion. It is remarkable how even today his influence can still move us towards the things of heaven. Sad to say, not all of us understand these spiritual values as well as we should, nor do we give them a proper place in our lives. Many of us, in fact, strongly attracted by sin, may look on these values as of little moment, even something of a nuisance, or we ignore them altogether. It is deeply rewarding for men striving for salvation to follow in Christ's footsteps and to obey God's commandments. If only everyone could learn this lesson from the example the Martin gave us.' (*Excerpt from the homily of Pope John XXIII on the canonization of St Martin de Porres 6th May 1962*).

Do not be afraid!

It can be hard to identify with someone like Martin, someone who seems to have been born holy. We can admire him but may find it difficult to see him as a model for our own lives. We can be tempted to create a saccharine version, to see him as an anomaly, someone who loved everyone and was so kind to animals that he could even speak to them, but not as someone whose life should be imitated. Not even all saints can speak to animals. But saints' lives always show us something; so what is it that Martin's life shows us? He shows us that God's grace can overcome everything. A boy who was poor and abandoned by his father, truly found his real father in heaven. A man who was despised and racially abused did not look to be admired, to be loved, to be served or to avenge the injustice he received. Instead he became Christ for others. He challenges us not to doubt that God's grace can do the same for us if we ask for it. The greatest commandment, as Christ said, is to love God with all our hearts and all our minds and all our strength and our neighbour as ourselves. He would not have commanded it if it were not possible. The life of

Martin de Porres shows that it is and, as John Paul II always told young people, we should not to be afraid to be saints.

Martin de Porres is the Patron of Inter-racial Brotherhood. His feast day is 3rd November.

Prayers to St Martin de Porres

Prayer for the intercession of St Martin

Most humble St Martin whose burning charity embraces all, but especially those who are sick, afflicted or in need, we turn to you for help in our present difficulties and we implore you to obtain for us from God health of soul and body, and in particular the favour we now ask.

(mention your intention).

May we, by imitating your charity and humility, find quiet and contentment all our days, and cheerful submission to God's holy will in all the trials and difficulties of life.

St Martin, pray for us.

Novena in honour of St Martin

First Day

St Martin, you learned from Our Lord to be gentle and humble of heart. You knew that happiness can only be found in surrendering to God's will.

Pray for me that I can too can become gentle and humble, finding happiness in trustful acceptance of God's will.

One decade of the rosary.

Second Day

St Martin, your love and gratitude towards God found expression in loving and serving your brothers.

Pray for me that I can come to know God's love for me and seek to be of service to my neighbour.

One decade of the rosary.

Third Day

St Martin, you were called 'Father of the Poor'.

Pray for me that I can learn to be generous with the gifts I have been given whether money, time or talent.

One decade of the rosary.

Fourth Day

St Martin, your ears and heart were open to the Word.

Pray for me to be given the grace to accept the gospel in faith and to live it to the full.

One decade of the rosary.

Fifth Day

St Martin, you had unshakeable trust in God's power and mercy.

Pray for me that I may always trust in God's love and care in all the events of my life.

One decade of the rosary.

Sixth Day

St Martin, you lived a life of prayer and God answered you in miraculous ways.

Pray for me that I may be granted a spirit of prayer.

One decade of the rosary.

Seventh Day

St Martin, you did the hardest and most menial of work with a cheerful and willing spirit.

Pray for me that I may understand the dignity of human labour and that I may do my work as if for God Himself.

One decade of the rosary.

Eighth Day

St Martin, you shared in Our Lord's redemptive suffering through acts of penance.

Pray for me that I may learn to offer the sufferings of my life for the salvation of the world.

One decade of the rosary.

Ninth Day

St Martin, you died a holy death surrounded by your brothers and full of hope of eternal life.

Pray for me that I may have this same grace.

One decade of the rosary.

Simple Novena to St Martin

Say for 9 days running:

St Martin de Porres,
Your concern and charity were so great
they embraced even the animals of the field.
You are an inspiring example;
hear the requests of your needy brother/sister:
    (mention your request).
By modelling our lives after yours
and imitating your virtues,
may we know that God has looked favourably on us.
And because this is so,
we can accept our crosses with strength and courage
and follow in the footsteps of Our Lord.
May we reach the Kingdom of Heaven
through the mercy of God,
Amen.

Prayer to St Martin, Apostle of Humility

Father, you have given us in your humble Son, Our
Lord, Jesus Christ,
the model of all virtue and perfection.
Grant us, we pray, the virtue of humility.
We think so little of you because we are so full
of ourselves.

We cannot love you until humility shows us our nothingness,
and makes us rejoice in our dependence on you.
You have given to the world a glorious apostle of humility: St Martin de Porres.
Guide us by his example and strengthen us through his intercession,
in our efforts to conform our hearts to that of your crucified Son.
May the glory of sainthood which you have bestowed on St Martin,
draw the world closer to you.
Renew in these days, O Lord, the wonders you performed
Through St Martin during his lifetime on earth.
Through the same Christ Our Lord.
Amen.

Traditional Prayer to St Martin

Most glorious Martin de Porres, whose burning charity embraced not only thy needy brethren, but also the very beasts of the field, splendid example of charity we hail thee and invoke thee! From the high throne which thou dost occupy, deign to listen to the supplications of thy needy brethren that, by imitating thy virtues, we may live contented in the

state in which God has placed us and carrying our
cross with courage and strength, we may follow in
the footsteps of Our Blessed Redeemer and his most
afflicted mother, that at last we may reach the
Kingdom of Heaven through the merits of Our Lord
Jesus Christ. Amen

Litany of St Martin

Lord, have mercy. *Christ, have mercy.*

Christ, hear us. *Christ, graciously hear us.*

God the Father, *have mercy on us.*

God the Son, *have mercy on us.*

God, the Holy Spirit, *have mercy on us.*

Holy Trinity, one God, *have mercy on us.*

Holy Mary, Queen of the rosary, *pray for us.*

St Martin, ever in the presence of God, *pray for us.*

St Martin, faithful servant of Christ, *pray for us.*

St Martin, lover of the Holy Eucharist, *pray for us.*

St Martin, devoted to Our Blessed Mother, *pray for us.*

St Martin, raised from the depths to be a heavenly man,
pray for us.

St Martin, honoured son of St Dominic, *pray for us.*

St Martin, lover of the most holy rosary, *pray for us.*

St Martin, apostle of mercy, *pray for us.*

St Martin, minister of charity, *pray for us.*

St Martin, miraculously conveyed to far-distant lands, *pray for us.*

St Martin, freed from the barriers of space and time, *pray for us.*

St Martin, seeking the conversion of sinners, *pray for us.*

St Martin, protector of the tempted and the repentant, *pray for us.*

St Martin, helper of souls in doubt and darkness, *pray for us.*

St Martin, compassionate to the sorrowful and afflicted, *pray for us.*

St Martin, consoler of the discouraged and the unfortunate, *pray for us.*

St Martin, peacemaker in all discord, *pray for us.*

St Martin, touched by all suffering, *pray for us.*

St Martin, comforter of the sick and the dying, *pray for us.*

St Martin, angel to hospitals and prisons, *pray for us.*

St Martin, worker of miraculous cures, *pray for us.*

St Martin, guardian of homeless children, *pray for us.*

St Martin, humbly concealing God-given powers, *pray for us.*

St Martin, devoted to holy poverty, *pray for us.*

St Martin, model of obedience, *pray for us*.

St Martin, lover of heroic penance, *pray for us*.

St Martin, strong in self-denial, *pray for us*.

St Martin, performing menial tasks with holy ardour, *pray for us*.

St Martin, patron of inter-racial brotherhood, *pray for us*.

St Martin, pray for us.
That we may be made worthy of the promises of Christ.

O God, exalter of the humble, who brought St Martin to your heavenly kingdom, grant that through his merits and intercession, we may so follow his example of humility on earth as to deserve to be exalted with him in heaven. Through Christ Our Lord, Amen.